Time Well Knows the Tides:

Kalends, Nones, and Ides

Monique Finley

DEDICATION

For Jenn,

Our journey has been an incredible adventure.

Thanks for traveling with me.

Contents

KALENDS

kalends, kalendae: *the first day of the Roman month**

** day of the new moon (Kalends), Roman priests*
announced the number of days to the
3ʳᵈ quarter (Nones) and full (Ides) moons.

We Exist In

Sacrifice, exhaustion, exasperation, exhilaration.
Emotions: quite simply, the state we exist in.
Tabulations, computations, abacus, calculus.
Mathematics: quite simply, the equation we exist in.
Hydrogen, carbon, oxygen, calcium.
Bodies: quite simply, the solution we exist as.

Products of the Mind, I

I. *To think; denken; cogitare*

Look, do you see?
There it is: reality.
Everywhere things:
idea action brings

mind to matter.
Thoughts scatter
to global winds.
Now, it begins:

a thought had,
a market fad.
This dog wagged.
Aristotle sagged.

Products of the Mind, II

II. *To play; spielen; ad ludere*

Bored people happen:
Google Map Pac Man.
Back now? Glad?
Donde es realidad?

Blended, extended,
and augmented
intuitive software
-oh, so, very rare-

seamlessly render
bits from sender
to cloud cuckooland.
To Aristophanes: a hand.

Products of the Mind, III

III. *To live; leben; vivere*

YOLO, young ones yell out
before opting for a new route.
No one can in D.C., drone.
What! No aerial dropped phone?

Instead, cyber biotech deal,
still delivered wonder weal.
Unintended consequence
like a film out of sequence.

Flowery golden Democrates,
proves the virtuous can tease,
can cause delayed reactions,
and hastily made retractions.

On Napping Along Side an Ancient Roman Road in Britania

There we slept. I imagine
like many before us.
Pilgrims

along for the day,
energized by the stones
placed

by some ancient unknowns,
ancient even to the Roman
builders

of this marked mile of stones,
where an old Roman road slept in
Avebury.

On an Insomniac's Napping

A budding habit must repeat regularly.
An established habit must repeat indefinitely.

I habitually napped.
I enjoyed the habit.

Something happened.
It was tragic.
I broke the habit

and napped no more.
An exhausted body
understands

no vow spoken,
no oath taken.

I crashed hard on
the couch despite

my broken habit.
Just once, no repeat,
in the clear, vow

intact, so I thought.
An exhausted body
understands

no vow spoken,
no oath taken.

A broken habit does not repeat.
A reestablished habit repeats indefinitely.

With No One to Blame

Oh man, what a crock it is
to have no one to blame.
No room to complain
when the last minute
revelation hits and you stop,
ya just quit, sit, and try
to forget. The pitcher is empty.
Not a drop, not a lick.
Nothing to slide down your
gullet to moisten the road thru
15ft of murky tests and scholastic
underachievements. Red tape
bureaucracy counting,
segregating, keeping hard copy.
Regardless the governmental
systems' built-in deficiencies,
there's no one to blame when
the pitcher is empty and you
were the last to pour a glass.

Blame A. Name

A baby boy born
quickly becomes
a scapegoat, such
is the luck of one
named: Blame.

Ah. Um, what does
it mean? A middle
initial? A signifier
meant to specify
one out of a lot.

And. His middle
initial meant: "And."
How can one blame
and not name? He
wasn't responsible.

Afterwards, the ban
on middle initials
began with forms
begging: "Please
write 'N.M.I. under

any block marked 'I.'
All requests comply
with the Privacy Act
 of 1976." None cared
enough to stop it.

Louisiana in My Blood

Ol' Louisiana in my blood,
I used to think only of SoCal
but now I'm not too sure.
That misleading paradise has had its ups and downs.

Poor Louisiana in my blood,
has gone round after round
with devastation and destruction.
That Who Dat crowd has had its ups and downs.

Swampy Louisiana in my blood,
no soft lil' kitten tangled long
with the beasts in Bisteneau.
That safety chain-link has had its ups and downs.

Cunning Louisiana in my blood,
not a missed step in political corruption
takes the cake on criminal induction.
That shady dealing state has had its ups and downs.

Spicy Louisiana in my blood,
Creole, Cajun, and everyone betwixt,
with a sexy south of Baton Rouge accent.
That Louisianan drawl has had its ups and downs.

Humid Louisiana in my blood,
I claim you as my birthright
and hold the stately honor high.
That Mardis Gras party has had its ups and downs.

Hot Louisiana in my blood,
I'm carrying my pride all the way
to that SoCal beach back in Avila Bay.
That cool Pacific Ocean has had its ups and downs.

A Little Beach in Galveston, Tx.

I first heard your name in '96.
Galveston.

I was fresh from the California shores
to the Louisiana swamps and I longed for
beach—any beach—in a way only those raised
with the sea can yearn for coastal sands.

We met not that year and I feared
I might never meet you. Galveston.

I first trucked your way in '04.
Galveston.

I was fresh out of the Navy seeking friends
long flown from the swamp lands.
And, when I saw your rocky shores and sands
full of seashells I knew the wait was worth it.

We met well that year and I seared.
I never bought sunblock, Galveston.

Swapping Freeways in Hollywood, Ca.

Nigh on a decade passed before I once again
beheld that white sign on the mountain side.
Rolling through concrete tides at 55,

I spied "HOL" but not "LYWOOD."
Spanish tiled villas and steel-beamed
condominiums blinded us from full view.

Round and down the mountain, graded 6.5,
weaving in and out of traffic praying the brakes
don't slide. We swap the 5 for the 10 then swap

freeways again. The 101 we ride, beyond the exit
for the Sunset Strip, where fans can see everyone
they wished to be. And, the sun sets on the fabulous.

To Walk or Run

Ambulate slowly—
a miserly gait—
waiting for some sign of fate?

No heed to speed—
Mach 1 tennies—
running for some late date?

Walkers gain
the panoramic view
while their running

compatriots gain
pavement pounding
narrow vision—

the Marxist each
according to their mission.

Doing the Duval Crawl in Key West, Fl.

No one does the Duval Crawl
quite like sailors out having a ball.
From Truman Annex they say,
"take a left at the clock,
don't go the wrong way."

As habit often dictates, I never listened.
I quickly found queens that glistened
in the neon night lights,
"how you doin' sweetie?
Come on in, it's alright."

What a ball I had without my Command,
that sorry lot would've been mad
if they'd known I took a right,
"a Yard Dog will set you
straight." I crawled all night.

Key West is more than a drink stop,
after all, Castro's but a skip, a hop.
Southern Most Point says,
"this is the closest we get,
Cuba's but 40 miles away."

In the Swelter

There you are, so close to me…
proximity.
Pulses mingling, nerves tingling…
electricity.

Burning.
See the sweat pouring?
Yearning.
Feel the heart fluttering?
Smarting.
Hear the ache pounding?
Parting.

There you were, so close to me…
inaccessibility.
Pulses singling, nerves stinging…
complicity.

O' sweet sweltering felicity
O' desirous deeds denied
to us by we:
you and me.

Across the Big Blue

Hung out Google style with my girl the other day,
was so excited the computer forgot what I had to say.
Couldn't share our thoughts in quick bursts,
they'd just get lost to the gremlins curse.
Started speaking like Captain Kirk,
was surprised to find Morse's code
still works. Echo bounced the wave
like Occupy's People's Mic.
"I'm ready" : "I'm ready"
"to visit" : "to visit"
"soon." : "soon."

It Doesn't Matter

It doesn't matter how well you plan,
though planning is important.
Last minute unforeseen details
force adaptability.

It doesn't matter how much you research,
though researching is important.
Last minute unforeseen minutiae
force contiguity.

It doesn't matter how well you prepare,
though preparing is important.
Last minute unforeseen disasters
force flexibility.

All that really matters?
Fortitude.

Hardy Stock

We come from hardy stock.

Cruel custodians of pragmatism,
beasts tamed by curiosity,
set loose by the possibilities,

armed with weapons of mass ignorance.

Defended by antipathetics
who misunderstood the starlight,
then sought to hold the cosmos –

criminals and heretics, everyone.

Difference Between Empty and Full

Some mouths receive less than enough
to eat
while their government pays
farmers to keep crops at bay.

Little emaciated beings with bloated bellies
imagine
while staring at bloated bureaucrats
unbuckling belts to give their done-laps

a break from the gourmet feast. Full on the wine
and rich
desserts, they chuckle over empty glasses
debating the next phase

of the fate of the nation and how to assist
the poor.
Hunger's the difference between
empty and full.

NONES

nones, nonae: *the fifth or seventh day of the Roman month**

** the Nones were on the fifth day,*
unless the month was March, May, July, or October

Aching, for One Whole Minute

Under the thunder and in the rain,
anointed by cold hard pain.

Don't it feel strange to hear your name
being called out by the insane?

Stomach rumbles, brain waves jumble
not intoxicated, still she stumbled.

A little shy butch, she mumbles,
before the night's through she bumbles.

Slip of the tongue, quit it Freud,
sometimes it's better to play Koi.

Fidelity

I don't want to stand here tempting you,
the thought lingering in your mind.
The shadow of doubt following you
as you wonder if you crossed some line.
Remember your world before, the goals,
the dreams you have: thinking of together,
forever, and how happy you'll be.
Circumstances change. It's been known to occur.
Don't fear what you don't know,
but know what you fear. Be prepared.
I'm standing here, watching you
(not stalking, no worries babe.)
Admire your loyalty, sworn faithfully.
Determined, chin cocked high, shoulders back,
chest proudly stuck out. Jettison all trepidation.
Life will lead you exactly where you need.
So, sit back hon, the rollercoaster's gaining ground.
There're ups and downs, twists and turns.
You'll bounce around, pride may bruise.
But, smile regardless. All of life is a gift.

The Neanderthal Within

Where does the rage come from?
No soft sounds, no gentle, "om."
It's more guttural than that,
a matter of scientific fact.

Within us: the keys, the codes,
the instructions for poetic odes
or violent destruction untold.
Hard-coded genes unseen, now sold

on HDTVs across the globe
free with purchase of parietal lobe.
Dr. Jekylls meet Mr. Hydes. My friends,
our battle is within. Thus, it ends.

Anger never did bode well. Hide
our Jekylls from the Hydes inside.
What else are friends and enemies for?
Drink to diseases – thirst for war!

To each as he pleases, Marx begged,
never knew bipeds to be octo-legged.
Such was his surprise when each took
more than their need, sharing forsook

in the name of hoarding, prepping.
Never care about lines – overstepping.
That's you and me – one bit Neanderthal
fighting our cry for the civilized. That is all.

O'Israel, Know Thou Not Palestine?

O' Israel, know thou not Palestine?
Are both not cultures with histories?
Two peoples spoilt over time entwined.

O' Palestine, know thou not Israel?
Aren't both but two of many stories?
One ebbed millennia, the other flowed.

O' Jacob, see your sons of Rachel
triumphantly trample demographics
true to geolocation, history skewed?

O' Philistia, art thou not a Philistine,
sent to end disputes via new tactics?
Prefer negotiation or continued feud?

Affairs of State

Who are these names and faces upon media portals?
These suited fools, too greedy to put their nation first?
These gimmicked, subliminal niceties, played for profit, worse
played for boredom of the elite degree, on and on, he chortles.

It is not what we were taught.
The fairy tale was life itself, wrought
with ups, downs, and verticals
they never bothered to tell us about.

Governments rise and fall, the game played by elites in long halls.
Even so, the people keep on keepin' on like nothing is wrong.
John Q. changes his tune when bombs fall – that's a new song.
That day, he marches, armed, crying about the dirges, funeral calls.

It is never what we're taught.
This fairy tale is life itself, wrought
with lefts, rights, and horizontals
they never tried to warn us about.

Environmental debates rang throughout the industrial lands.
They impacted the mountains, polluted rivers, marshes,
then denied the evidence of their eyes, shouting harshest
that there is no proof, while pointing with contaminated hands.

Power Realized

Power realized volumes of emotion
hung teetering
on the abysmal edge of
power realized.

He whooped gleefully,
"By the power of…"
in the mirror he mouthed
"me."

And, there he stared,
casually laughing hysterically at
the tip-of-balance as
Power leaned—first left,

then right—realizing power
fluctuation as half his reflection
vanished
from his narrowed sight.

Power realized myriad life
hung teetering
on the dismal edge of
power realized.

He pondered, greedily,
"No power greater than…"
in the mirror he mimed,
"me."

In his darkest moment,
fanatically chortling frantically
balanced by the tip-of-his-nose
Power realized

limitless power.

Upon Seeing Our Stuff Gone

My heart skipped, something was missing.
Not just one thing, but all the important things.
Wait. That car. Those men.
They didn't? They did!

Air gone. Lungs uncooperative.
Breathing mechanisms have failed me.
They took...no, they didn't.
Yes. Yes, they really did.

They got it all. All those years of work.
My novel. My poems. My anguish.
My knees hurt. I can't stand.
How did they? Does it matter?

Someone, look at the cameras.
Tell me your cameras work.
I don't understand. How did they...
Call the police. Call them quickly.

They took our ID, our money.
My cigar box of memories.
My lost loved ones – stolen.
Your notes, your mementos – gone.

Sodium Drops

Sodium drops roll down epidermis.
Beads build before gravity
feels the pull down, down,
the sodium drops roll.

It isn't the hot.
It couldn't be the cold.
Must be the over-exertion
of a tormented soul.

Mixing Good and Evil

Hundreds pressed into a mob forcing
themselves further into the thick
of civil disobedience.

Voices formed a current of explosive
energy chanting:
"No Justice. No Peace."

As if so simple a black and white
picture ever existed in the realm
of humanity.

It matters not their cause;
it matters not their reasons
for joining together heedless of seasons:

Good does evil once determined by the just
while evil does good to impress the rest
of genuine good-standing.

Rushing to Drone

Hide the truth behind the lies,
the propaganda disguises, and
the fools, whose anger—without
discernment—burns cities down.

Target anyone in the streets,
where civilian and insurgent
blend so perfectly—ignorance
becomes the cry—that weapons
dropped speak of dead innocence.

If only mainstream media covered
the disgusting depths, the reality
of glitches made from "unmanned"
planes dropping death from the skies
like some ancient gods bent on global
destruction. Oh, wait. They do. What's

the going rate for a UAV pilot?
Better a terrorist captures a drone
than another American not make
it home from places we've no right
to be. Though, I'll tell you honestly,

it makes me nervous—knowing.
We seem to be crashing drones
with too much regularity for me
not to scream, "TAKE HEED."

(Tomorrow, it could be your backyard).

Targets of the Watch List

It's getting hotter every day.
"Global warming," scientists say.
"Rising temperatures," sweat drips
down a cynic's smirking lips.

No rise can out shine the sun.
Consequences can't be out run.

Save the individual. Sacrifice the state.
Some things shouldn't be up for debate.
Save the self to sacrifice the group.
Or, save the whole, prep the young troop.

Is no loss worth putting up a fight?
Another poor kid dies tonight.

United, we are all and one.
Divided, we sacrifice any one.
Any can become the chosen
who falters at the thought, frozen

to the spot where life meets death.
A mirror shows no bated breath.

Hated, he waited until she was sated.
No fault of his own, it was fated,
he'd protect her from the coming storm.
Together, they dared to never conform.

Labeled extremists. Assumed terrorists.
Arrested, being targets of the Watch List.

Playing Games in San Diego, Ca.

Sweet sunny San Diego,
as a girl I used to dream of you.
I'd hear the tales of ocean vistas
and the best damn pizzas

but, it's the games you played
that stole my heart away.
Had me begging for more
stories of your glorious shores.

To young me, you were mythical lands
hosting athletes and their devout fans.
I vaguely knew of your killer whale,
compared to X Games 3 & 4 it paled.

In 2000, while on leave from the Navy
I finally had an opportunity
to partake of your pleasantries
as I drove through the palm-y Palisades

trying to make my way to the main gate
before the tank ran out of fumes. Fate
has a cruel streak and humor wild.
When I saw the gas station I smiled,

even so, the car stuttered then faltered.
Flashers on, traffic rerouted, I roistered
the whole two blocks to that gas station.
Naught but two gas cans full caused elation.

Some say it's the destination, not the trip.
To them I say, please get a grip.
For me there's no comparison
after all, my journey led to a garrison.

Never Won

The West was never won.
Façade of an old buildin',
in an abandoned town
where the Gold Rush fled in
the Oil Boom's wake, like dogs
runnin' from hurricanes bleedin'
salt on wounded marsh bogs.

We never won the War to End Wars.
Instead, touched off the greatest threat –
the atomized affectation of stars
harnessed for the long haul – let
us master space, that last stellar
hope of cybernauts in mass debt.
A group of astropunks burn out a car,

protesting, "no war is ever won.
Reach for the stars. Burn away
the scars on the land. Pass the sun
rays this way. Stellar peace, a new day."
They cover our scars with starlight.
We all know there is another way –
lay down the blanket – Starry Night.

Violent protestors never won
the concessions that they sought.
With progress history is undone,
against the consequences they fought.
Do we make or break the spy drones,
flying subsidies our taxes bought?
Ignore it all, we've got smart phones.

Catchin' Up

Atomic seconds accelerate and decelerate under the strain of perception. Our conceptualizations mold our realities on an ever-changing basis, input-output on repeat ad infinitum until we short out and stiffen up. And, in between the screaming "me, me." We're all just catchin' up, never truly makin' up, thus we're ever behind. Knockin' back interest on some piece of crap that depreciated the second we drove off in it. How're we supposed to break even in a system designed to create debtors out of nations? Out of nations? There's no catchin' up when the govie's charged interest on money it's supposed to create from nothing. Nothing. Nature demands fluctuations occur when increasing the money supply. Since 1913, the FRB's been charging tax on Uncle Sam's dime. Double tax like double jeopardy in double time, double mint, double mint, dumb. It ain't capitalism we're watching die, it's cronyism. Supply-side economics tells the financial sector merchants need customers, capitalism reasons, ain't no reason to bite the hand that feeds. "Crony capitalists" are code words for 20th century aristocrats waging private wars across sales territories—real countries—divvied up and parceled off to recent college graduates caught between the promises of legacy educations and the stark realities of living in the age of service workers, code for "indentured servants" (a.k.a. wage slaves). Now, you're caught up, don't get caught up in the gossip, the lip service, the entertainment, the very things meant to distract from the high-handed devious BS that's plaguing every countryside worldwide.

Upon My Furrowed Brow

So much I never understood.
  Circular-logic like feedback loops.
  "H-O-R-S-E" when shooting "hoops."
Why do the vulgar hate the crude?

Twitch of the eyelid, faster now.
  'Cause of sorrow wonders, "why?"
  Never quit causing sorrow, I espy.
Why stagnate in negativity's row?

Perception and reality—remote-views.
  Ignoring truths, the lies espoused.
  From slumber, the mores aroused.
Learned the ruse, evaluated the news.

Actions, not words, always heard.
  Cycles and seasons, unending repeat.
  Dance to victory, trudge to defeat.
Climb back on the horse that reared.

Nothing comes at the other side.
  Quality is made of excrement.
  All that matters: time well spent.
So, why live like you already died?

To Dissenters, All Dissenters

You grasp hold of truth so tightly
it seems you might drop it. Relax.
A truth found, can never be lost,
maybe misplaced for a time, never
lost. It takes courage, unbound
courage to step forward holding
up naked truth. Never fear your
words aren't getting through, look
left, right, left, truth is marching
toward you, for you, forward with you.
Ever on, like those saints, or ants,
one-by-one, hurrah, hurrah. Those
self-evident truths people still die
for and kill over…yeah, those are
dreams we're still trying to grasp
through the wisps of this nightmare
someone mislabeled civilization.

Regarding Pastiche

At the behest of a challenge—three years,
results as yet unknown—I sat down with
a teacher's text (msg)—prompting a text
some twenty pages long—as yet unfinished.

From a few transmitted words I found
a tale that must emerge utilizing "pastiche."
"WTF is that?" I wondered pleasantly.
Once I understood the concept, I eagerly

engaged the task. Cocky, full of smarminess,
having successfully turned the last text into
a single sentence story. That triumph, Jack's
single-serving friend, pounded me down,

page after lyrical page. A pastiche, in epic
ballad form, about a dentist arriving in a post-
nuclear kingdom hell bent on keeping up with
appearances. Oh, how beautifully the words

flowed through me to the computer—out
of ether into ethernet—via my keyboard, saved
on an 180GB HDD hidden somewhere under
the plastic of my now broken laptop. It took

some time for my finances to align, but
eventually I purchased the equipment needed
to free a nearly finished epic ballad born from
a text sent in the 21st century and nearly lost

to all eternity before it ever met its own ending.
Now, if I could just reach that muse, that
whispering wind that swirled in, I'll need her
if we ever want to know how this epic ends.

On Stein's Word Games

I must protest. Protest must I.
I find no lesson to be learnt.
No learned lesson do I find

from games a woman played
with herself. How she toyed,
"a woman has a cow…" How!

That phrase today would spark
outrage in feminist circles.
Rantings comparing a woman

to a bovine…How heifer-esque
you look today, my dear general,
Gertrude. I wonder if the script

writers of *The Simpsons* knew
the truth when they made Bart
spew, "Don't have a cow, man!"

Unless…but, wait…what more
could "cow" possibly stand for?
O.

IDES

ides, ideae: *the thirteenth or fifteenth day of the Roman month**

** the Ides fell on the full moon, the ancient Romans
were familiar with the associated lunacy*

Unto Caesar? Eh, Brute?

"O' great Caesar,
do you feel the knife
in your back?"

Brutus asked as
he plunged the knife
in deeper still.

Ever that sudden
realization: frienemy's
sneak attack?

Some just don't
back, quite like they
should - eh, Brute?

"Eheu, is that you
my dear frienemy,
my dear Brutus?"

Caesar asked as
he lay impaled, blood
pooling 'neath him.

An Angel's Sigh: One Lost, One Last

How easily the sounds escape, the last breath,
last words spoken on an angel's sigh:
now, it's just I. No more is it you…
you and I. No. Now it's just I.

    I scream as the beat of wings
    sing your praises to ancient sages.
    I cry out in vain as the pain
    stains your face, one last trace.

Too easily the sounds escape, the lost tears,
lost fears, spoken on an angel's sigh:
now, it's just I. No more is it you…
you and I. No. Now, it's just I.

    And, I scream as the beat of wings
    sing your praises to ancient sages.
    And, I cry out in vain as the pain
    stains your face with that last trace.

One last breath, one last word to knock away
one last tear, spilt, I fear, for an angel's sigh:
now, it's just I. No more is it you…
you and I. No. Now, it's just I.

Self-Deprivation

The art of depriving
as if lacking could be formed
with two hands.

Will: the power of
thought, action, creation,
labor of lands.

Deprive self of coy
toys, the ignorant joys
slip like sands.

Pick a future bold
with that in mind, other
things withhold.

Whittle down effects,
keep the irreplaceable,
sell everything else.

With little to your
name, there's less to pull you
into the fold.

That which is unique
in you is that which is unique
to the whole world.

The mantras, dogmas,
karmas, weren't meant to harm
us, they hearld

tidings simple
as peace, love, a gentle
dove's wings wide.

Specter Woman

Feel your cold hand caress my cheek—
shivering suddenly.

Hear your voice whispering my name—
eye about suspiciously.

Press our lips, in disbelief, yet so real—
heart catches instantly.

But...
you're not even...

here.

No Greater Impact

"A child doesn't understand death,"
some adults speak, laying a wreath
upon memories of friends—gone.
Empathetic, a child weeps alone,

afraid to exert needs on folks
caught up in knells and polk
salads. A wake, like potluck,
mingles unlikely sorts; pluck

and plume, feuds resume twixt
petty rivals recalling hits, licks
received by a kid in another age;
at sight, the anger, the old rage.

A child understands tragedy
befalls with chaotic trajectory.
Preventable accidents: Darwinesque,
drunk driving while sending a text.

Maestro Danny

A greeting louder than nails on chalkboards—
a puppy chorus in full howl—
greeting the mistress of the house.

Maestro, Danny, the little reddish-brown
one-eyed tank conducts the orchestra
in one last canine chorus line.

The door barely shut when an image flashed
of sunglasses and car keys left on the couch.
Sneakily, like a ninja kitty, the door cracked open

one last again. The maestro she caught in the act
with a chorus that didn't get the clue.
How quiet now the maestro's dead—too quiet now.

Heavy Cloak of Hereafter

Incandescence illuminated the somber room
So much the better to lighten the gloomy atmosphere.
The mood was grim. Spirits low. Tears freely flowed.
"How?" asked gravity impaired faces. Few bothered with why,

knowing no remedy to the irresistible conclusion
that is without doubt the harsh finality of existence.
Ours is the light road of here-and-now
traveled under the heavy cloak of hereafter.

Rodin's Tabula Rasa

Rodin's hotel-turned-museum must have
been a glorious sight long before fate
snubbed Rodin's life.

Countless feet tramp up his stairs leaving
dirty crumbs in wooden slat cracks.
While bungling limbs usher bipeds

through the various display rooms.
Thousands of the curious make the trip
just to trip over fanny-packed viewers

equipped with individual telescopic digital
eyes held to the center of their foreheads—
seems innocently Cyclopes-esque—

though the truth be known few care to really grasp
the full spectacle of a herd moving through the house.
Wipe their lenses clean, this is but a tourists' *tabula rasa.*

Expanding Universe Theory

A limited opportunity
exists for observation.

If astrophysicists
hypothesize correctly,
then eventually

the very skies
will alter before
the collective eyes

of humanity (should
we survive ourselves).
What does it mean? To

know that even the
cosmos are subject
to life, death,

and sudden
impacts?
What does it mean? To

know in perpetuity
the cosmos will be
empty? Neptune's

lost—the black—
no star guides.

Perched on a Projectile

We send them up in controlled burns,
just a handful of our finest
chosen to perch on top

of a projectile weapon.
They cut through the sky
leaving behind scorched concrete,

a trail of white, and all earthly concerns.
Theirs is a tin can life
making adjustments for pitch and roll

beyond the atmosphere
of the orb they call home.
Out of this world matters not one bit,

'cause even an astronaut's taxes
come due on April's Ides.
Fortunately, IRS gurus

grant extensions
and "off the planet" is still
a good enough reason.

Someday we'll up and down
with such frequency
the gov will eradicate

the "off-planet" excuse,
thus, denying extensions
on balances past due.

Holding onto Selves

What're you to me, me to you?
In the dissonance, a dataset is misplaced.

A parched esophagus in the liquid
refreshment aisle: plethora of decisions.

Uncontaminated H2O will suffice.
Self-collection devices confiscated.

Per capita, we're bureaucratic chattel.

Fines issued by insolent governments
intent on auctioning our inheritance.

Questions mar one courageous enough –
ask why – get an iron boot to the throat.

Protest? Mask. Protesting veils? Unmask.
What're they to us, us to them?

Per capita, we're bureaucratic chattel.

Slowly, time brings the wellspring dews
the news of radically progressive changes.

Daily, the collective acts on the system,
compliant or not, as each deems right.

They are us. We are them. Thus, they and
we are everything to each other. See us?

Rest in Peaces

"I like modern plumbing," she confessed,
while protestors stormed city streets.
Slowly she undressed,
    ready for a peaceful night's rest.

Brimming with desires suppressed,
while forcing smiles, they impressed.
Each morning they wake,
    wages not life at stake.

"I like modern technology," he confessed,
while dissenters occupied city streets.
He quickly undressed
    ready for a peaceful night's rest.